Mary Brancker
CBE FRCVS

Memories of her life and work

Recollections of Mary Brancker brought together by her friends in August 2014, the month which would have seen her 100th birthday.

Mary Brancker: Memories of Her Life and Work published by the Independent Conservation and Wildlife Society (known as tza).

Edited by Rowena Johnson

Design by Richard and Ruth Corrall

Published by Brand 29

Copyright © 2015

www.tza.org.uk

Contents

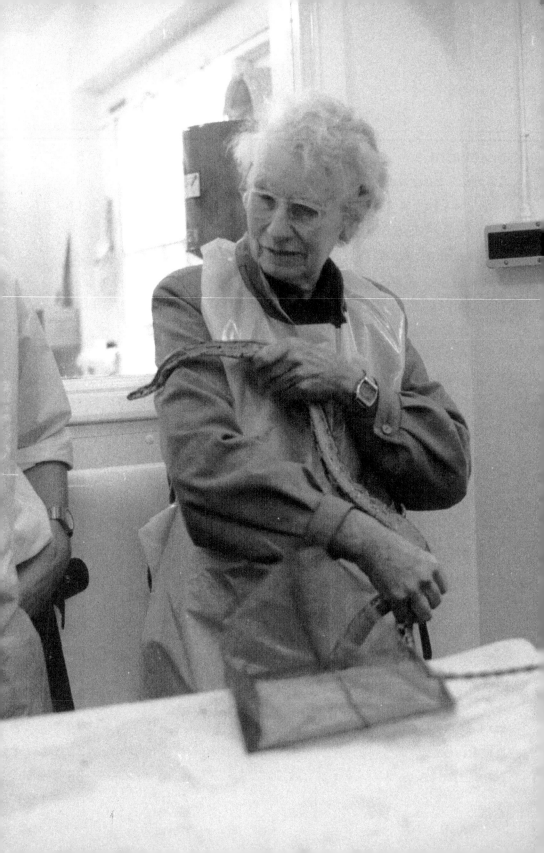

Foreword

When Mary celebrated her 90th birthday in August 2004, her volunteer friends and colleagues in the Twycross Zoo Association (TZA), now the Independent Conservation and Wildlife Society (known as tza) gave her a surprise birthday party. Mary was invited to Twycross Zoo to attend a 'thank you event' for the volunteers and she gave Ivan Ellis quite a glare when she realised, after a brief sentence of thanks to the volunteers for all their hard work throughout the year, that the rest of the event was a birthday party for her! Very quickly Ivan and the rest of us were forgiven though and Mary enjoyed herself so much that she asked for another party to celebrate her 100th.

When we all came together with great sadness at Mary's funeral in July 2010, we decided that we would still hold a party in Mary's honour in August 2014.

At the beginning of 2013, it was realised that preparations must begin or we would miss the important date. A sub-committee was formed from the Independent Conservation and Wildlife Society with Ivan Ellis as the Chairman. We approached Twycross Zoo to hold the event there, as a central place that all who knew Mary from various areas could reach. As we discussed what form the event should take, contacted and talked to people, and gathered information and memories about Mary's life, we soon realised that 'just a party' would not do justice to Mary or our memories of her. We had already made plans to establish a Mary Brancker Bursary, to offer students on animal courses small grants, for travel or research materials required to complete their dissertations and it was decided to promote this further at the event.

Finally, on Sunday 17th August 2014, over 70 of Mary's friends gathered at Twycross Zoo. We re-dedicated the Mary Brancker Waterways and then in 'Windows on the Wild', we listened to memories of Mary, ate, laughed and had a wonderful afternoon in each other's company.
Belinda Bird, known as Belle, Chairman of tza, opened the proceedings with a welcome speech explaining that two sessions of talks had been

arranged with refreshments in the middle, and tea and celebration cake after closing remarks and thanks by Vernon Russell, Treasurer of tza.

Over the many months of planning for the event on 17th August 2014, it became clear that there were numerous memories of Mary from all aspects of her energetic fulfilled life. It was decided, therefore that we would publish this book, recording the speeches from the day, but also outlining in a short biographical section, the main events of Mary's life and other memories of her that were not included on the day.

While we were doing the research for the biography my daughter, Ruth, contacted Sue Bradley, who has been kind enough to send us her memories of working with Mary on the autobiographical recordings that Mary made during the last 18 months of her life. Sue had approached Mary to be the first interviewee in what is now a partnership oral history project between RCVS Knowledge (formerly the Royal College of Veterinary Surgeons Charitable Trust) and Newcastle University's Centre for Rural Economy, with the British Library as the archive partner. Mary, of course, responded to this invitation with characteristic enthusiasm and almost 25 hours of recordings about her life were made. Sue was impressed by Mary's business-like approach to the recordings as well as being taken to lunch before the work began! Details of where this recording can be heard are included in the Resources section at the end of the book. I am sure that Mary was thrilled to have been the pioneer contributor to this successful and worthwhile project.

I hope that we have done justice to Mary and managed to capture both the essence of her charismatic personality and the atmosphere of our enjoyable day together in August 2014. I have tried to be as accurate as possible but memories differ and it has been hard to be sure of some dates and details. I apologise if you feel that I have not recorded your memories of Mary correctly and also that it has taken so long to put this book together. I am sure you will appreciate that it has been very difficult to draw this work to a close.

I hope that the book will give people great pleasure in reading and remembering this wonderful person and friend.

Rowena Johnson
January 2015

Thanks and Acknowledgements

Our grateful thanks go to everyone who was kind enough to send us their memories of Mary in response to our appeal last year. Particularly to those who then agreed to give a speech on the day or to read other's contributions for us and those who gave us permission to publish their memories and photographs.

To Penny and Paul Nicholson for so kindly supplying us with a wealth of archive material and coming to our assistance later, by sending us the originals, when our copies were not clear enough to publish. Also for all their help with the copyright details and finding alternative pictures that we could include.

To Twycross Zoo for supplying the plaques required to re-dedicate the Mary Brancker Waterways on the 17th August. To their catering company, who were marvellous on the day, providing a beautifully dressed room and wonderful food; Alma and her staff could not have been more attentive and helpful.

To Brooksby Melton College for helping us to set up the Mary Brancker Bursary and to their staff who spoke on the day to outline the details of this ongoing fund.

To all the members of the Independent Conservation and Wildlife Society for their support, particularly the members of the subcommittee who planned the event and to everyone who helped on the day to ensure all present enjoyed the day.

Our thanks go to Ivan and Jo Ellis, who worked tirelessly from the time that we first started planning the event and have continued to help with the writing and proofreading of this book.

Particular thanks to Ivan Ellis for organising the order of speakers and for being the Master of Ceremonies on the day and ensuring that everything ran like clockwork.

To Belle Bird, Chairman of tza, for all her help, including the opening speech and to Vernon Russell, Treasurer of tza, for all his help and the closing vote of thanks.

To James Bayley, who knew Mary when she was the zoo vet, for creating two beautiful large flower arrangements and a number of smaller ones. Red roses were Mary's favourite flowers and the arrangements certainly did her proud.

To Clare Bailey for the stunning cake.

To Mark Ellis, Ivan Ellis, David Bird and Chris Johnson, for taking photographs on the day and to Tim Ellis and Ivan Ellis who have given us copyright permission to use many of their other photographs.

Finally, my very grateful thanks to Ruth and Richard Corrall who have worked so hard to organise, research, typeset and publish this book for us. Without their invaluable help our aim of recording these memories would not have been achieved.

Rowena Johnson
January 2015

Mary's Life: A Timeline

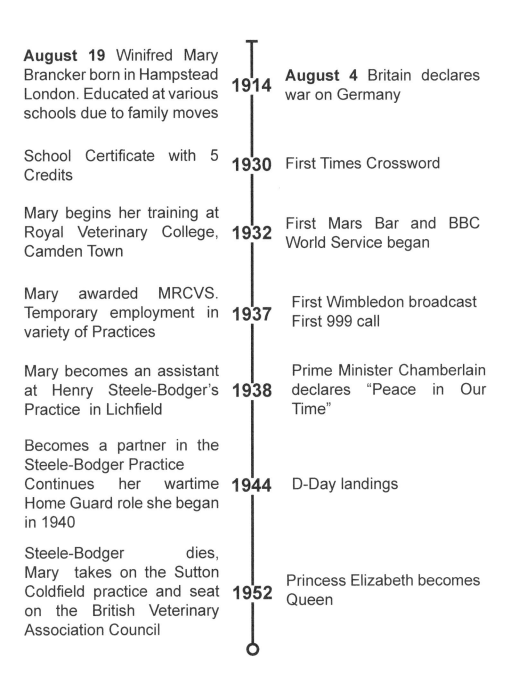

August 19 Winifred Mary Brancker born in Hampstead London. Educated at various schools due to family moves

1914   **August 4** Britain declares war on Germany

School Certificate with 5 Credits

1930   First Times Crossword

Mary begins her training at Royal Veterinary College, Camden Town

1932   First Mars Bar and BBC World Service began

Mary awarded MRCVS. Temporary employment in variety of Practices

1937   First Wimbledon broadcast First 999 call

Mary becomes an assistant at Henry Steele-Bodger's Practice in Lichfield

1938   Prime Minister Chamberlain declares "Peace in Our Time"

Becomes a partner in the Steele-Bodger Practice Continues her wartime Home Guard role she began in 1940

1944   D-Day landings

Steele-Bodger dies, Mary takes on the Sutton Coldfield practice and seat on the British Veterinary Association Council

1952   Princess Elizabeth becomes Queen

Twycross Zoo opens Mary becomes the Zoo Vet	**1963**	Worst winter since 1947, ground is frozen from January to April
Becomes Junior Vice-President of British Veterinary Association	**1966**	TV broadcasts in colour England wins World Cup
Mary becomes President of the British Veterinary Association (first woman to hold this position). Directed operations during the Foot and Mouth disease outbreak. Awarded OBE	**1967** **1968** **1969**	Breathalyser introduced Outbreak of Foot and Mouth Disease: 4,300,000 animals slaughtered Abortion legalised in Britain Man landed on the Moon
Directed the veterinary developments in fish farming	**1970**	North Sea Oil discovered
Member (till 1984) of Royal College of Veterinary Surgeons Council	**1971**	Kingsway Mersey Tunnel opens
Published All Creatures Great and Small: Veterinary Surgery as a Career	**1972**	Munich Olympic disaster
Mary granted Honorary Fellowship of the Royal College of Veterinary Surgeons	**1977**	Queen celebrates her Silver Jubilee

Retires from general practice	**1984**	£1 note withdrawn
Elected President of the Twycross Zoo Association Awarded the Dalrymple-Champneys Cup and Medal by the British Veterinary Association	**1985**	Miners' strikes end
Becomes a Fellow of the Royal Veterinary College	**1989**	Hillsborough disaster
Given Honorary Doctorate from Stirling University	**1996**	First woman jockey in the Derby
Awarded CBE. Described as 'Icon of the Century' by Tony Blair	**2000**	Millennium celebrations take place around the world
Royal Veterinary College open Mary Brancker House, student accommodation BVA award Mary the Chiron Award	**2005**	Hunting with dogs banned in England and Wales
Waterways Exhibit opened at Twycross and dedicated to Mary Brancker	**2007**	Smoking ban in public places in England
July 18 Winifred Mary Brancker died	**2010**	General Election and Coalition Government, first since WWII

Mary's Life: A Short Biography
Mary as we knew her

Mary Brancker was born on the 19th August 1914, the same month that the First World War broke out. The second daughter and third child of Henry Brancker and his wife Caroline, she was christened Winifred Mary, but she always introduced herself as Mary and was known within the family and their circle of friends as Polly. Research has shown that her mother was Winifred Caroline and her older sister was christened Caroline Antoinette and her brother, known as Paul, as Henry Paul.

Almost immediately after Mary's birth, her two older siblings, Antoinette and Paul, became quite ill with an infectious disease, and Mrs Brancker feared for the health and indeed life of her newborn daughter. Their family doctor reassured her that the newborn was a "tough specimen" who would survive in the "bottom of a ditch if necessary". While Mary was still under five, presumably the same family doctor suggested that she would do best on food that could be "passed through a sieve". Over the next 95 years, Mary was to prove this family doctor a wise man in many ways. She was a tough specimen, who did have health problems, such as requiring major back surgery when this was an even more difficult procedure than it is now, but she was always determined to fight her way back to good health, following to the end of her life the daily exercises needed to keep her back supple.

The family story of "food to be passed through a sieve" was handed down to Mary without the details of why the doctor had advocated this, but the retelling of it always made us smile, at the Appleby Inn after a day of volunteering. Mary, then in her 90's, would consult the menu in great detail, listen to what was available from the specials board, and then with her mischievous grin, order "soup please". She never enquired what type of soup it was, but always seemed to enjoy her meal. Perhaps again the doctor was proved correct and in later years, as in childhood, her digestive system could not cope with large meals later in the day.

During the year that Mary was seven, the entire family was invited to look round Shackleton's ship, as he prepared for his next (and final) trip to Antarctica. Her father had met Shackleton when he worked in Argentina, they became great friends and although she was only young, she could remember quite a few details of that exciting day.

The Branckers were a forward thinking family, who believed in educating girls as well as boys and both the older children were sent away to boarding school before they were eleven. Teaching Mary however, must have proved slightly more difficult, because she would talk about going to a number of small, presumably local private schools, where she would spend hours drawing what she described as 'o's' and 'j's'. Over the years of course, she passed exams and proved that she was neither slow or unteachable but it was possible that she had initially felt she was both.

While still going to school from home, Mary felt that she had been very unjustly treated on one occasion by her mother. The family system would appear to have been that if a child was not well enough to go to school, they returned to bed for the day. On the day in question, however, Mary had returned to bed, but her mother came upstairs a little later on and read the riot-act. Mary, when retelling this story, pronounced that she had been very unfairly treated, there was nothing in the agreement about being told off, but she admitted that if she had known what would happen, she would have gone to school! Mrs Brancker obviously knew her younger daughter very well!

Mary's father was to die when she was still seven years old, and her mother was left with very little income, which had to be used as wisely as possible. Determined that Paul would continue at boarding school, Mrs Brancker wrote to Antoinette's headmistress to say that the family were moving to a smaller house in the country and that her daughter would not return to school the following term, as they could not afford the fees. Luckily the headmistress was a very enlightened lady who replied that Antoinette would continue her schooling with them. A couple of years later Antoinette returned home at the end of term with a letter from the school to say that Mary would be able to start the following term, also without charge. Mary was unable to recall exactly where the school was, but talked about learning to swim in the North Sea and we think that the school would have been on the Suffolk coast.

A few years later when Mary was of an age to think of her future, she was home from boarding school, perhaps with a bad back as she was laid up in bed, when the Headmistress sent through a list of suitable, and now possible, vocations for her to consider. She would recall that her mother came into her bedroom with the list, which ran to around a dozen career options for young women in the 1930's. Her mother read the list aloud, to which she answered "no" to each suggestion. Fixing Mary with a stern look, Mrs Brancker declared "I will read the list again, slowly". Mary recalled that to become a veterinarian was the only one which appealed to her so she answered "yes" to this, presumably the last choice on the alphabetical list. Mary really wanted to be a farmer, but in those days that was only possible if there was either land or money in the family, preferably both, but in the Brancker family neither of these were available.

Mary remained grateful to her headmistress for that list of suitable careers all her life, compiled by a women who was enlightened enough to appreciate the wealth of opportunities which were opening up for young women in the early decades of the twentieth century, both in the universities and colleges. Mary had a much wider choice than most young women would have been offered. She also recognised that she could so easily have missed out on being educated, but for the kindness of the headmistress in waiving the fees. Throughout her life, Mary did everything she could to encourage all young people to take full advantage of the educational opportunities offered to them. She particularly advocated training to be a vet, of course, especially for girls, but was quite happy if they chose other careers as long as they fulfilled their potential and gained the best qualifications they could.

There seems to have been between seven and ten girls enrolled at the Royal Veterinary College to begin their veterinary course with Mary in 1932 when she was 18. The college had been pleased to welcome female students a few years earlier, as they brought with them publicity and welcome funding. They had begun a replacement building programme, and as Mary was to remain at the College until 1937, she was still there when the new buildings opened. One of the earliest female students, Olga Uvarov qualified from the College in 1934 and was to go on to be the first female President of The Royal College of Veterinary Surgeons (RCVS).

Mary enjoyed her five years in London, although she was very short of funds and it is thought that her sister may have contributed towards her living expenses from her own wages. Mary walked to save bus fares and was generally as careful as possible to live within her limited means.

Mary had a number of happy memories of college that she enjoyed recalling, one of which was when they got bored with books and went to visit the blacksmith in the College grounds. He once allowed Mary to make a shoe and put it on a horse, however she conceded that this was probably because the horse was due to be euthanased the following day. Horses were in fact the main subjects of the teaching for aspiring vets in Mary's day. At the time, horses were essential for transport and agriculture.

The story most remembered from this period of Mary's life, is about the elephant from London Zoo. Mary recalled coming downstairs into the main quadrangle at the veterinary college to find all the senior lecturers and professors gathered around an elephant, which had been walked down, by the keeper from the zoo, for a diagnosis. All went well for a while, until the elephant took exception to being prodded and examined by so many people, whipping round at great speed, it charged through the entrance arch of the college and set off back down the road towards the zoo! Being a member of a very intelligent species, the elephant knew the way back to its enclosure and was not waiting for the keeper, who running along behind, was not able to keep up, so jumped on the step of a passing bus. There cannot be many instances of bus drivers being asked to "follow that elephant"!

During the time that Mary was on her course, she ran a Brownie pack as Brown Owl. In those days, the Guiding Association rules stated that to hold a licence to take girls on pack holidays, a woman must be 21 years or over. Being a late summer baby, Mary would not be able to have her licence in time for the arranged holiday dates in the summer of 1935. Nothing daunted, Mary wrote to Girl Guide HQ, explaining that she had been born three weeks later than her expected date, and so should have been 21 at the beginning of August! Her argument was accepted and her licence arrived in time for the girls to have their holiday. Only Mary would have thought of that line of argument, never mind achieved a successful result!

Mary also spent time on farms and in general practice during the holidays to broaden her knowledge. She worked with cows in Wales, pigs in Suffolk and was fortunate enough to work with Bill Blount, who was known to be the only vet in the UK who was an expert on poultry. Later in his career Bill would became President of the British Veterinary Association (BVA), and was also Vice President of the World Poultry Science Association.

It is thought that Mary was one of only 21 students to pass the course, out of the 80 plus who began with her five years earlier.

Once qualified, however, she had a difficult time finding a job. This was partially because she was a woman, although Mary recalled that the opposition to women holding positions in practice often came from the wives of the vets, rather than the vets themselves! There was also some concern about a woman's ability to carry out the job, particularly from farmers who were worried about women being injured or needing help managing the animals.

Eventually, Mary was offered a job in London. Unfortunately, the position never materialised and Mary must have felt she was back to square one. She then obtained employment in Bexhill, but due to the loss of a contract she was let go after only a couple of months. Finally, a temporary job as an assistant was offered to cover sickness, at the practice of the eminent Harry (Henry) Steele-Bodger in the Midlands. By now it was 1938 and the practice was based in Lichfield with a branch in Tamworth. Later they would open a branch in Sutton Coldfield which Mary would run and eventually own but she began her job at the Tamworth branch.

A third of the practice work was connected with farming, the primary industry of the area at that time. Mary started to specialise in chickens, along with the domestic animals that made up the rest of the practice's work.

Harry Steele-Bodger was a veterinarian of distinction and became President of the National Veterinary Association (a precursor to the BVA) during the war. The Association's office relocated to Harry's Lichfield practice and remained there for the rest of the war. This led to some interesting evenings for Mary, who recalled driving through the blackout to collect and return to the station, senior officials from the Ministry of Agriculture, who came to Lichfield to discuss war arrangements with the veterinary professionals.

Between 1938 and the end of the war in 1945, Mary would go from being a junior member of the Steele-Bodger practice, to firmly setting the foundations of the dedicated, committed career path that she would follow for the rest of her life.

As the farmers were tasked with the necessity of producing as much food as possible at home for the increasingly besieged nation, their need of vets to help maintain the health of their animals increased. So did the workload, as some of the young, able-bodied male vets enlisted. Later in the war, many of the remaining men would be sent to the Far East to look after the horses, leaving only the older vets and the group of young qualified women to work as Mary would say, "round the clock". Her mother was living with her in the later war years and would get upset at having to take phone calls and wake Mary in the night when she knew that Mary had only just returned from the last job and was in great need of sleep. Mary was to say later that in addition to the immense volume of work, they also never had enough to eat, in the later years of the war. She was grateful to those farmers who would make her a meal after she had finished dealing with the animals she had been called out to, or would send her on her way to her next job with food in her hand.

At the start of the war, Mary also volunteered to serve as an ARP (Air Raid Precautions) officer and was in the Mounted Home Guard based in Sutton Park. Mary was also appointed to the National Air Raid Precautions for Animals Committee. This body helped to reunite animals with their owners or find them new homes after their own had been bombed. A picture of the card appointing Mary to this position and authorising her to carry out the work is in the Archives section towards the end of this book. Mary also received authorisation from both Staffordshire and Warwickshire police forces, for her to slaughter animals found injured or distressed. Pictures of these letters are also in the Archives section.

In 1942, Mary and her family received the awful news that her brother Paul had been killed over the Dutch coast. He was a Flying Officer in the RAF during the war. He had won the Distinguished Flying Cross as a result of his efforts in 1941, and then the Bar in January 1942, when he played a key role in a low level attack on an enemy aerodrome at

Herdla, Norway. Three months after this, Paul lost his life when his aircraft was shot down attacking an airfield in Holland. Although not frequently spoken of, Mary felt the loss of her only brother keenly.

During the war years, various non-essential activities were able to continue because they provided relaxation, which improved morale. The most important of these from Mary's point of view were the dog shows which she attended in the Midlands. It was at these shows that she became acquainted with Miss Molly Badham and Miss Nathalie Evans. The three ladies would remain colleagues in the post-war years, Mary becoming the first vet at the zoo that Miss Badham and Miss Evans started in 1963.

After the war, Mary became a partner in the Steele-Bodger practice, moving to the Sutton Coldfield branch. Harry Steele-Bodger died quite young in the early 1950's and Mary took over both the Sutton Coldfield practice and his seat on the British Veterinary Association Council.

Miss Molly Badham and Miss Nathalie Evans, although sharing cars to save petrol during the war to attend the dog shows, had originally been rival pet shop owners in Sutton Coldfield. This state of affairs continued after the war until they realised that they were dividing the pet shop market in Sutton and it would be more sensible to join forces and have one shop in the town. The shop was successful and the two ladies began to keep primates successfully, although not to sell as pets. Frighteningly, various primates were readily available for purchase in those days, although clearly unsuitable as domestic pets. The thinking at the time was that as apes and monkeys came from warm climates, they must be kept in warm, often humid atmospheres but like us, they would contract colds or pneumonia, often not surviving. Miss Badham and Miss Evans kept their first chimps in the flat above the shop, taking them for walks in the fresh air, and they thrived.

Mary delighted in telling people of the story when one day Miss Badham and Miss Evans came home to find the chimps had opened a window and were hurling the contents of the flat into the street. After this incident they decided to move to a bungalow in Hints village near Tamworth, which had a room suitable for the chimps to live in. This was in 1954 and they became the first people to realise that chimps, and other primates, would thrive outside in enclosures on grass. They took on a number of distressed animals and ones which had been seized at

Customs and it became known that if a sick primate was lucky enough to arrive at Hints, it stood a very good chance of surviving. This was costly, however, as often Miss Badham and Miss Evans had to buy the animal from the dealer in order to save its life.

Local people still recall how their families would take a Sunday afternoon walk to Hints village, in the hope of seeing the animals in the garden. By 1962 however, this sightseeing had become too big a problem for the small lanes in Hints village as people from further afield started driving over and parking their car near the bungalow. Miss Badham and Miss Evans decided that it was time to move the animals to a larger location. After the awful winter of 1962/63, when the ground did not thaw from Christmas until Easter, the official opening of Twycross Zoo was delayed until the Whitsun holiday weekend. Henry Evans, Miss Evan's brother, had struggled all spring to build the enclosures required to house the Hints animals and Miss Badham and Miss Evans moved into the house known as Norton Grange. This had been built as a vicarage but had not been lived in for many years. After the incredibly cold winter, in a house without central heating, and with a shortage of electric power to the site, the early months at Norton Grange must have been very uncomfortable for the owners of the newly opened Twycross Zoo.

Mary, having looked after the pet shop animals and later the increasing variety of primates at Hints, founded in 1961 in conjunction with the few other vets dealing with zoo animals, the British Veterinary Zoological Society, a branch of the British Veterinary Association. The aims of the founder members of the BVZS were to promote veterinary knowledge and skills to give proper welfare and healthcare to non-domestic animals. The BVZS would encourage all owners of exotic animals to use and exchange veterinary knowledge and also advocated suitable living conditions for these animals.

In autumn 1966 Mary was elected to the role of Junior Vice-President for the BVA, leading to a letter of congratulations being sent from a Mr Bowden. He must have been a good friend as the letter reads "Congratulations on your election as Junior Vice-President of the BVA. You have created history in being the first woman to hold this position, and I hasten to express the confidence which I place in you. This causes me some embarrassment as in addition to your charm and beauty I now have to concede that you have a modicum of brain". A copy of this letter is reproduced in the Archives.

Following her year as Junior Vice-President, Mary became, in 1967, the first woman President of the BVA and as it turned out, the only female President in the twentieth century. Mary was to go down to London to the inauguration of the second female President, Freda Scott-Park, in 2005.

She had a particularly difficult year as President, due to an outbreak of Foot and Mouth disease, the worst outbreak seen at the time. She was in charge of organising the veterinary response to the disease, which included having to slaughter many thousands of animals.

Following Mary's very difficult year as BVA President, she was awarded the OBE in 1969, in recognition of her work managing the Foot and Mouth outbreak.

Mary also encountered problems when the BVA President was invited to attend the annual conference of the Norwegian Veterinary Association, along with delegates from all over Europe; they were totally nonplussed when the British President turned out to be a woman, the only female delegate from all the vets across Europe. Mary was used to holding her ground and joined in the conference activities, which included a look around Oslo and a visit to their war memorial. Walking round this, she found her brother's name, which she knew was honoured there. Pointing to Paul Brancker (D.F.C and Bar) she informed those present that he was her brother. The attitude of the conference delegates and the organisers changed completely and she was able to represent the BVA as their President and to fully participate in the conference discussions.

In 1972, Mary wrote a book about her experiences as a female vet. It was entitled All Creatures Great and Small: Veterinary Surgery as a Career (My Life & My Work), and was published on the same day as the James Herriot book with the same title! They had an amicable discussion and neither minded about the complete coincidence.

Mary was founder member or President of many societies and organisations and her dedication and work was recognised with a number of awards and honours.

From the British Veterinary Zoological Society came the Zebra Foundation for Veterinary Zoological Research. Mary had a passion for research throughout her life and this foundation was set up with the object of assisting veterinary students and veterinary surgeons extend their knowledge and gain additional experience. The Foundation is still meeting this aim, with grants given out to students to further their knowledge and a number of published research papers have resulted from this.

Mary's involvement with the BVA opened many doors, including the opportunity to become involved with the growing commercial fish farm industry. Mary identified that research into veterinary care for fish farms was required, particularly to address the issues with eye care. Mary's contributions resulted in Stirling University obtaining funding from the Nuffield Foundation, allowing it to open an aquaculture research facility, now the world renowned Institute of Aquaculture. Mary continued for years with visits to Grimsby and Scotland to collect halibut eyes for research. Her involvement in this area led to an Honorary Doctorate from Stirling University in 1996.

Invertebrates were another passion of Mary's, although she always acknowledged that she was not fond of spiders, and had never knowingly touched one. When asked on the radio once how you tell if an invertebrate is unwell, she replied along the lines of "at the breakfast table, a husband or wife can instinctively tell if their partner is unwell and it is the same with invertebrates. If you are aware of their normal habits and health you can immediately tell when something is amiss." Mary started the Veterinary Invertebrate Society during the 1970s, recognising that veterinary knowledge of how to treat invertebrates needed to be improved.

The Society of Women Veterinarians, which Mary had founded in 1941, was wound up in 1990, as Mary felt the aim of the society, to further the progression of women vets within the profession, had been achieved.

Between 1971 and 1984, Mary also served on the Council of the Royal College of Veterinary Surgeons. In 1984, Mary retired from the RCVS Council, and also decided to retire from general practice. As she did this, she became president of the British Veterinary Nursing Association.

In 1977, Mary's contribution to the profession was recognised when she received Honorary Fellowship of the RCVS. In 1981 she was elected a life member of the BVA. She was also made a Fellow of the Royal Veterinary College where she had studied.

Mary was also a member of a number of other societies, including the Society of Practicing Veterinary Surgeons (Midland Counties Division), the British Small Animal Veterinary Society, and the Pig Veterinary Society. Mary served as President of Sutton Coldfield and District Dog Training Club and served on the Young Farmers' Club advisory committee.

One of Mary's lifelong interests was in tortoises, and she was an active member of the British Chelonia Society, which is involved with tortoise, terrapin and turtle care and conservation. She also kept tortoises for many years.

In addition to her involvement in veterinary and animal societies, Mary was a long-term member of the Sutton Coldfield Soroptomists, having helped to found the local branch in the mid 1940s. The Soroptomists started Kelvey House, a retirement home for impecunious women.

In 1985, Mary received the Dalrymple-Champneys Cup and Medal, which is awarded by the BVA for work of outstanding merit.

In 2000, Mary was honoured with a CBE, of which she was very proud.

The Chiron Award, given to those who have given 'Outstanding contributions to veterinary science or outstanding services to the veterinary profession judged in either case as being of a calibre commanding international or interprofessional recognition' was given to her by the BVA in 2005. Also in 2005, the Royal Veterinary College named its new student accommodation facility the 'Mary Brancker House' in her honour.

Mary became President of and a volunteer with the Twycross Zoo Association in 1985 and was one of the most dedicated volunteers. She retired as their President in 2001 but continued with her volunteer duties until just a few weeks before she died.

In 1997, the BVA held a 'Branckerfest' for all those many members who had been influenced or stimulated by Mary, celebrating Mary's 60 veterinary years. The 'Branckerfest' was a full day of papers giving a flavour of Mary's breadth of involvement in veterinary science (the Obituary in the July 2010 Veterinary Record has more details, see Resources at the end of this book).

For Mary's 90th birthday in 2009, she decided a flying lesson would be in order. Never one for convention, or slowing down in later years!

On 18th July 2010, Mary's long, fulfilling and influential life came to an end. Her influence, her work and her passion for animals and people will never be forgotten.

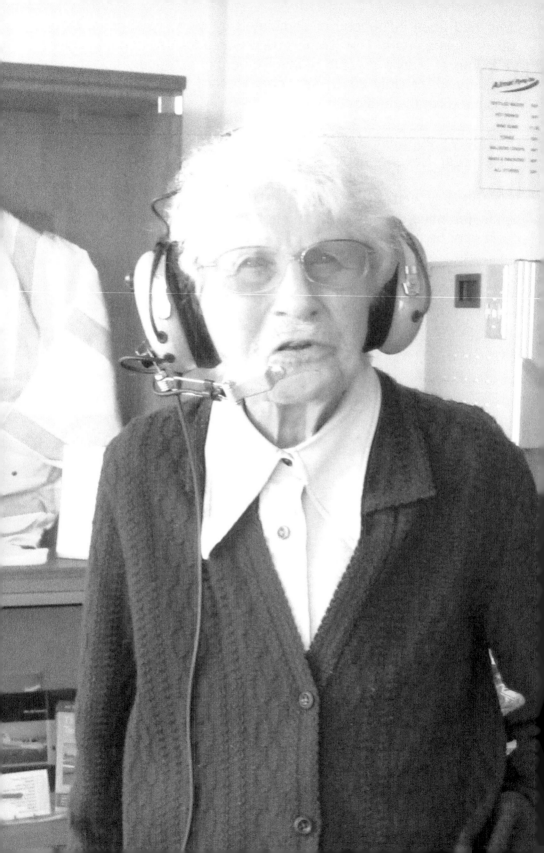

Re-dedication of the Mary Brancker Waterways

Good afternoon, I wish, today, that I was 2 inches taller, 4 stones heavier and had a beard. If that was so, I would match in stature Brian Blessed who, some 7 years ago dedicated this area as the Mary Brancker Waterways. He and Mary, shall we say, got on fine. Brian flirted with Mary and she responded with good humour. His final words to Mary when he left were "We shall meet again Mary, maybe in Heaven, but it will be pure lust!"

However, I feel that I knew Mary a little more than Brian. Mary and I spent many hours over coffee and chocolate biscuits chatting about 'this, that and the other.' I was also a Trustee and a TZA Volunteer alongside Mary.

Mary was the zoo vet for Molly Badham and Nathalie Evans at Twycross for some 23 years, and several years before that in Sutton Coldfield at their pet shop, and to their sidelines of dog breeding.

She was often at the zoo and was a familiar figure, and 'old' keepers would worship the ground she walked upon. Molly and Nat appreciated her too, although like any ladies who shared a kitchen, they did not always agree. But, animals always came first.

Mary was a valued Trustee of the zoo for many years, and again, her wisdom and knowledge were put to good use.

She later became a valued and enthusiastic TZA Volunteer, trained to help the visitors appreciate the work of the zoo. Her last duty was only three weeks before her stroke just short of her 96th birthday.

In 2007 it was felt by the zoo that her work and legacy should be commemorated in some way; naming part of the zoo after her. The then, newly constructed Waterways exhibit was an ideal chance to do this; Mary was delighted and agreed. One member of the staff declared in a loud voice that "You are usually dead when things are named after you." Mary was amused when she was told about that.

Mary, your name will live on for many years; we have here one such remembrance. Some of your many friends are here today to remember you. At the first dedication many then present only knew a name, and saw what appeared to be an elderly lady with white hair. They didn't know you Mary, we do.

I am delighted to re-dedicate these Waterways in your name, surrounded by your friends and colleagues, and Mary we all have happy memories of you.... And coffee and biscuits please.

Ivan Ellis

28

Memories from Ivan Ellis

My history with Mary began in the 1960's when I walked into the vets carrying Tiggs, my cat. Standing behind a table was a stern looking lady. This stern lady became a caring and professional lady, stroking and talking to Tiggs, and then she looked at me and explained what she thought was wrong and what she would do. Alas, Tiggs didn't make it (no fault of Mary's… it was cancer).

A little later I became a member of the newly formed Twycross Zoo Association (TZA) and I felt happy that MY vet was the vet at Twycross. For my sins I became the secretary of the TZA and the committee asked me to approach Miss Brancker about becoming our President.

I asked her, she looked at me, and said that she would do so, providing that she could simply be a figurehead and that she would not be expected to do anything. I agreed to this, reporting back to the committee that all was well, we had a President.

It was about three weeks later when, out of courtesy, I mentioned to President Brancker that we, the TZA, would be holding a home made cake stall in the zoo to raise money towards the Chimp House Fund. "Oh dear," was her reply, "I'm no cook, but if I bought a cake that looked as if it was home made would that be in order?" Mary duly turned up with a cake, she stood by the table… perhaps two hours later she said, "That was fun, do you do other things?" We explained what we did and what we didn't do. From then on she became more and more involved.

Part of the work we did involved helping the Education Department with exhibitions and visitor talks. Eventually we started what was to become a highly successful and famous Santa's Grotto. Guess who quickly got involved… President Brancker.

She busied herself with decorating Christmas Trees and sorting out Christmas lights, because, as she frequently said, she had no skills. Once up and running, she was happy serving teas and greeting children as they left Santa, encouraging them to open their presents (even if their parents didn't want them to!) She would greet tiny ones with a clap of hands and a 'Brrrrrr' sound. She loved it, so did the children! More than once we would find Mary crawling on all fours playing with the presents and children; the children aged 4 to 9, Mary aged 83/4/5/6…

As we progressed with our work, we trained for at least three days each year so that we would not let the zoo down. Mary, like the rest of us, took part in this and she was proud when she earned the right to wear our distinctive volunteer uniform. She worked at least twice a month, more if we were busy with projects. Anything but a figure head President. Her last duty was about three weeks before her stroke which in turn led to a swift loss of a valued member.

Several times during the year she would say that she thought it was about time we met for a chocolate biscuit and coffee. Jo, my wife, and I would arrive at Mary's about 10:30, coffee and a long chat followed, with chocolate biscuits of course. We chatted about affairs of the day, zoo matters, TZA things, people we both knew, vet experiences, lots of things. It was by now 12:30 or even later and as we stood up to take our leave Mary would say "Let's have lunch in Sutton Park." We duly had lunch in the park and afterwards returned for a four o'clock cuppa, finally leaving about 5:30. A good 'morning coffee break', and was always recommended!

Over the years, Mary and I, and at times others, would put the world to rights. We discussed matters zoological, and more than once we re-organised the zoo, not just Twycross, but all zoos.

She repeatedly told us all that she had no skills, and at school she spent a lot of time filling in 'o's' on pages of papers or books. As a former teacher I cannot condone this, but looking as positively as possible, this exercise would increase hand and eye co-ordination, and letter recognition. As a veterinary surgeon, hand and eye co-ordination were, of course, pretty vital.

When in the USA, she and a lady of about the same age were sitting on a seat, or log, over looking the Grand Canyon. A car stopped just past them and an American jumped out with a camera. "Oh," said Mary, "let's move so that you can get a good photograph of the view." "Gee Ma'am, I don't want the view, I want a shot of two sweet old ladies looking at the view." Mary was amused.

Mary often related the story of the feisty chimp and the injection technique. The chimp was a bit of a handful and needed an injection for something or other. It was decided that the deed would be done in one of rooms in the house, which was the private house of Molly Badham and Nat Evans. They would hold the chimp, an arm and a leg each, whilst Mary would inject. The scene was set. The feisty chimp was trapped; Mary prepared the syringe… "Miss Badham, Miss Evans, an emergency…" at this crucial point Molly and Nat hurtled through the door, closing it behind them of course, to attend to the emergency. Mary froze with the syringe in her hand some four feet away from a strong willed chimpanzee. Some five minutes later, emergency over presumably, the door opened a tiny crack and a voice said, "Mary, are you alright?" "Oh yes," said Mary. "The chimp and I came to an agreement; we would keep still until you returned." The procedure then continued!

One evening, quite late, her phone rang. She answered it and a child's voice said, "Come quick, Daisy's calving". The phone went dead. Mmmm, thought Mary, child... cow...Daisy...calving...I know who that is. Off she went, and yes, she knew which farm to go to. She knew her flock, or in this case, her herd!

She always had time for people, she would listen and nod wisely, how often did we all find her so helpful? How many acts of kindness did she give us all? She could be a bit naughty at times, but her kindness and helpfulness will never be forgotten.

You know, for a lady without skills, who filled 'o's' in at school, she didn't do too badly. It must have been a tremendous effort to get a place on a Veterinary Course as a lady in those far off days. The lady without skills somehow made the grade, managing to get a job, managing to run her own Practice, and she won the hearts of the Veterinary Society and was elected as President, the first lady to do so. Awarded a CBE and an Honorary Doctorate degree. Not bad for a lady of no skills.

The TZA members and Volunteers remember Mary well, and one of our members expressed our thoughts in a letter she sent to me on hearing that Mary had died. "Mary was full of life, she was fun, full of knowledge, humour, grace, warmth, curiosity, intellect, assertiveness, modesty, wisdom, acceptance, respect and as such we will remember her with love, affection and admiration for ever. It has been a privilege to have been a friend."

At the turn of the century, Tony Blair, then Prime Minister, published a list of 'Icons of the 20th Century'. One of these was Miss Winifred Mary Brancker, and who would doubt this accolade. It was with amusement to me that she appeared between Henry Cooper, the heavyweight boxer, and Stirling Moss, the Formula One driver.

One other thing to mention about Mary is the Bursary tza has set up in her name. We are helping students in their final exam year by providing money to help with their projects and theses. She would very much approve of this.

Miss Brancker, Miss B, 'The Boss', Aggie Moo, Coudah, Mary, Icon of the last century, valued friend and colleague – here's to you!

Memories from Pauline Manfield

Pauline, a good friend of Mary's from Sutton Coldfield, began her talk by explaining how she first met Mary as the vet who worked hard over two years to prolong the life of her dog Honey. Honey started with mammary cancer soon after Pauline had given the retired guide dog brood bitch a home and Mary operated a number of times during the final two years of this lovely dog's life.

Mary was later to call upon Pauline's help on a number of occasions. Pauline, a paediatrician by profession, was asked to listen to Louis' heart when Mary had detected he had a heart murmur. Louis was one of the first chimpanzees to be born at Twycross Zoo and Mary was concerned that he would need an operation in order to lead a long and full life. Pauline, with her experiences of listening to young human hearts was thankfully able to reassure Mary that Louis' murmur was not life threatening.

Later Mary rang Pauline when on a cold icy day she had fallen and hurt her elbow. Being Mary she had carried on with her work but when back at her surgery had x-rayed her arm. Seeing where the damage was, she rang Pauline for assistance. Pauline arranged for an orthopaedic surgeon to meet Mary in A and E but Mary was not happy at having to stay in the hospital until the next day when the operation could be done. She only agreed when it was explained to her that a bed may not be available if she went home overnight.

In 1978, Pauline told Mary that she was buying a house. Mary immediately assumed this was to give Pauline's two Burmese kittens a garden to play in, which they did not have at her flat. In fact, the house was to accommodate Pauline's parents! Of course, it did have the added benefit of a garden for the kittens.

In 1995, Pauline's dentist, Barrie Taylor, offered her a cabin in a yacht called Emeralda that he had hired to visit the Galapagos. Mary was the person invited to go with Pauline to share the cabin. The yacht held twelve people and they flew first to Quito then onto the Galapagos, landing at the smallest airport Pauline had ever seen.

Their cabin held bunk beds and although the ladder looked very difficult to use, Mary was quite happy to have the top bunk bed and coped with it with no problems throughout the holiday. They had a naturalist on board who guided them to the best areas and they had an amazing holiday seeing many different species and the trip included an across-the-equator ceremony.

Not long after the trip, friends of Pauline offered to arrange a holiday to Botswana and Mary again happily accepted an invitation to accompany them. The organiser was initially concerned that Mary, then aged 81, might find the trip too much but she was quite able to do her share of the driving and enjoyed seeing all the different animals.

On being confronted by threatening looking elephants near the road, Mary's sensible advice was "to drive away – quickly"! The only time Mary was not happy was on the journey home when an air hostess asked her if she required assistance at Heathrow!

In her late 80's, Mary broke her hip. As this happened near to Christmas, Pauline invited Mary to spend Christmas with her before facing the journey south to convalesce with Penny and Paul. However, Mary recovered so quickly that she stayed with Pauline before Christmas and was able to go to Penny and Paul's as planned for the festive season!

Mary was again able to help Pauline when the cat she was looking after for a friend on a long holiday went into renal failure. Between them they managed to keep the very elderly Burmese cat alive until she could return to her own home for the last few months of her life.

Pauline ended her talk by saying that she felt privileged to have been accepted as one of Mary's friends. She will always remember Mary's stories of delivering lambs in cold open fields, of the fish farming research in Scotland and the shock of hearing Mary's distinctive voice unexpectedly on the radio during the 1967/68 foot and mouth problems.

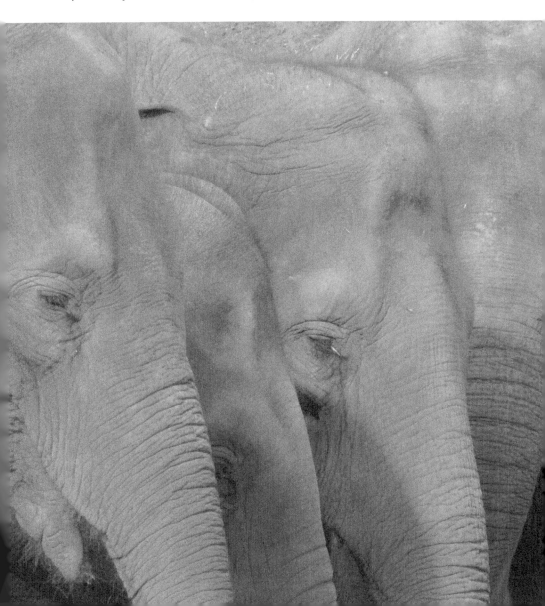

Memories from Roger Coley

Roger began his talk by reading a piece sent by John and Margaret Cooper from JFK airport as they travelled to Puerto Rico to give a series of lectures so could not be with us on the 17th August. They felt that Mary would be amused that they were still visiting interesting places at their age to lecture to veterinary associations at annual conventions.
They wished us a happy and memorable event and included with their message the tribute which John himself and a colleague, Peter Holt, wrote at the time of Mary's death for the Veterinary Record of July 24th 2010.

Roger then went on to outline how he met Mary and came subsequently to be her successor as the vet at Twycross Zoo. They first met when he was working as the vet at Drayton Manor Zoo. Mary was the veterinary surgeon designated by the Home Office to inspect the zoo; he remembers Mary as a 'real live wire' with a great sense of humour, very keen mind, and excellent common sense. She arrived at the zoo for the inspection wearing sensible, flat shoes and had a very purposeful walk that was difficult to keep up with. Roger acknowledged that he immediately fell under Mary's spell and they got on 'like a house on fire'. The zoo got a satisfactory licence and Roger met her at subsequent inspections at Drayton Manor.

A few years later, he was very surprised to get a phone call from Mary. She had decided that she wished to retire, and wanted to know if Roger would be interested in being her successor as vet at Twycross Zoo. Rather taken back, Roger replied that he knew very little about either primates or reptiles, but Mary assured him that this would not be a problem.

Mary had already spoken to Roger's partners and they had agreed to allow Roger to shadow Mary at Twycross one day a week for six months. Mary felt that would give Roger time to become accustomed to the very different clinical approach to zoo animals. Roger, unable to believe his luck, said that he would be delighted to accept this offer, and they began meeting the following week.

Mary taught Roger 'huge amounts about zoos, zoo animals, the politics of the zoo world and life in general'! Her breadth of knowledge and understanding of human and animal nature was exceptional.

Roger accompanied Mary to meetings in London of the small number of vets working in zoos and learnt a lot from these people but just as much from Mary, and about Mary, on the train journeys home. He recalled a number of instances from her early life with the vets at Tamworth and Sutton, eg. the pig sprayer riding his bicycle between farms, injecting pigs with an antibacterial purple dye which resulted in vaguely blue-pink pigs!

Roger also told of the AA man on the Mile Oak Crossroads, who used to stop traffic to let her through. Possibly for their safety!

Her father, who was a close friend of Shackleton, the explorer, died while she was at school, leaving the family somewhat impecunious. The head mistress of her school insisted that Mary joined her sister in the school, and educated them both free of charge.

Mary went on to be one of the first women to enter university and graduate as a vet.

After Mary retired, she continued to accompany Roger to vet meetings throughout the country. On one journey to Chester, with Roger driving, he suddenly realised that they were 40 miles north of their destination, because they had been talking too much!

A few years later, while on a visit to Gerald Durrell's Jersey Zoo, it was obvious that a female orang had recognised Mary. She had been born at Twycross and had been moved by the RAF between the two zoos. While they were standing near the orang enclosure, the female orang started trying to push woodwool through the enclosure fence. The nearest vets tried to take it but it was pulled back, several times, but when Mary stepped forward the orang let her take the wool.

After retiring as a zoo vet, Mary worked in many areas of the profession including the Veterinary Fish Society. She became involved in trying to find out why the halibut fish farming in Scotland was largely unsuccessful, as the fish developed cataracts. Mary would drive to the north of Scotland, collect halibut eyes and bring them to a veterinary eye specialist. There was little money available so I doubt she was ever paid.

Roger finished by saying that he felt that Mary was an amazing asset to the veterinary profession as President to the Association during the foot and mouth outbreak in the late 60's, when Mary was influential in ensuring that enough vets were available to control the outbreak.

Mary is missed by many people both inside and outside the profession, for her insight and 'joie de vive'. It was a privilege to work with her and also with her tortoises.

Memories from Barbara Brittain (Brit)

I first knew Mary as Zoo Vet and President of TZA, when she finally gave up driving I became her chauffeur on journeys to and from the Zoo on meeting days and when volunteering. It was during these journeys that I really got to know Mary, listening to her many stories.

On the occasion of her surprise ninetieth Birthday Party, I was given instructions to pick Mary up as usual but to arrive a little late so that everyone else was already there. That bit was easy but on the return journey Mary insisted on taking all the balloons with her so my car was full of balloons and so was the hall of her house when we arrived home.

On Bank Holidays TZA would often hold a Book Sale; Mary, Iris and myself were detailed to run this in the Napier Centre sharing the building with Wildlife Artist, Paul Dyson, who often held exhibitions at the Zoo. Paul needed coffee, every hour on the hour, so Paul, Iris and myself would take it in turns to make the coffee in the kitchen of the centre. On one occasion Mary decided that it was her turn so off she went. It was a very wet and windy day and Mary seemed to be missing for ages, just as we were thinking of sending out a search party a very wet and wind blown Mary appeared with the coffee. Instead of using the kitchen she had been all the way to the Gorilla Outpost Café.

Whether she was known as Mary, Polly, Miss B, Aggie Moo or the Boss she was the same person and was loved and admired by all.

Memories from Jean Green

Miss Brancker – 'The Boss' or 'Miss B', as she was known by her staff, was the veterinary equivalent of TV's Barbara Woodhouse.

To Miss B, the owners were an occupational hazard as she treated pets first and the owners second. She was adamant that the clients always held their animal correctly before she examined them, even if it took them ten minutes of instruction to get them to comply. Even now, clients will comment that she used to scare them to death, but they all say that they liked and respected her. She had a wicked sense of humour and a bad driving record, and often the two went together.

One particular story she used to tell was from after she retired from general practice (i.e. she was no spring chicken!), and she was going up the M6 to visit Blackpool Zoo. It was fairly early in the morning with not much traffic and Mary said that she had been driving for about half an hour when she was pulled over by a patrol car with blue flashing lights. She stopped her car on the hard shoulder and a young policeman approached her car. She wound down the window, he took one look at her and, obviously surprised by her age, said "Madame, do you know what speed you were doing?". To which Mary replied, "Yes young man, 98 miles per hour"! After, she said, a lovely chat with the officer, he apologised as he gave her a speeding ticket. She said that as he was so good looking and polite, she took it in good grace.

You always knew when Miss B had arrived at the veterinary surgery at 63 Lichfield Road. The garage was under the surgery and she used to drive in at such speed, that she always hit the front garage wall, shaking the foundations of the house! The staff used to look at each other, nod and say "the boss has arrived!"

After she retired, she had yearly practice reunions at Twycross Zoo, and even in her twilight years it was head down to try and keep up with her. She knew most of the animals, especially the primates, by name, and most of them recognised her, even to the point that when some of them saw her they picked up handfuls of poo and pelted her with it – what fun!!

Miss B had a deep affection and respect for her staff, as they did for her and this was shown as most stayed in her employment until she retired.

She was an old school vet, unlike most modern vets, at the end of the day, if you had done a good job, she always said "thank you" which meant everything to us – her staff.

Memories from Samantha Cawthorn

Aggie Moo, as she was known by my family, was a longstanding family friend so when my mother moved back into Sutton Coldfield in the early 70's with her 18 month old daughter, to escape an abusive husband, Mary Brancker was the first person to offer her a job as a live-in caretaker at her Lichfield Road Practice. I was that daughter and from then on my childhood was magical. Unable to pronounce 'Aunty Mary' my garbled toddler dialect translated it to Aggie Moo and as Aggie Moo it has stuck, with cards and letters always being signed by Aggie Moo. Aggie Moo became a second grandmother to me who I saw daily for the first 10 years of my life.

Later, when I had children of my own, it became clear to me that she delighted in small children as much as she did in the animals she treated. My memories are filled with having tea parties with her beloved tortoises when they came to stay, one of which was called Granny, as a visiting child had said to her that it's wrinkled neck reminded them of their granny, which Aggie Moo thought was hilarious! The tortoises had party hats and music and behaved terribly, trampling over their plates of party food. Aggie Moo, again amused by my comment of this, wrote a letter of apology on behalf of her tortoises for their sad lack of party manners.

Aggie Moo seemed to attract tortoises at that time: I remember her having one that had been saved after a client had accidentally ran over it with the newly introduced flymos, rather than putting it to sleep she mended it's shell with a type of cement, which worked perfectly. Another tortoise was brought in by an agitated client saying he wanted it put to sleep as it had given his daughter worms – refusing to listen to Aggie Moo's explanation that this wasn't possible, and working himself up into a steam, she continued to charge him double for the task, and then passed the tortoise into my care where he lived a very happy life for years after!

I also remember being allowed to creep very silently into the recovery room once to see what I thought was a tiny baby lion cub. Why it had been operated on at the surgery and not at Twycross I don't know. The recovery room, on the floor below my bedroom, was always a box of delights and having proved myself trustworthy I was allowed a free range of the surgery and other rooms, after surgery hours had finished. More often than not, there would be some sort of small animal recovering quietly, who would delight in the attention of a small visitor. Not always but occasionally it would be a more exotic animal from the zoo. I remember monkeys and parrots passing through. At that time, the PG Tips chimps were celebrities in their own right and I always hoped that they would pay us a visit and I would open the door to find them pouring tea!

Year after year, Aggie Moo tried to hatch tortoise eggs in her incubator in this room. Unfortunately our cat Tiggy thought that this was a deluxe litter tray! Again, rather than being angry, she took Tiggy's side and said that she didn't blame him!

Aggie Moo was always full of stories from the zoo and the animals she visited – how the monkey who remembered her as the lady who gave injections always hid his head in the straw when she came in, to no avail as she needed to inject his behind! And the gorilla who always remembered her and whom she counted as a friend. Being a vet wasn't just a job to her, it was her life, and one that she was fiercely committed to. The animals always came first as far as I saw, and in later years I remember many heated discussions being had when her partner at the time, Rowland, would argue that they needed to charge more. From what I can remember as long as it covered the cost of the medicine and surgery overheads she was happy – she most certainly wasn't in it to make a profit.

Aggie Moo stood up for animal rights and funnily enough, I can't look at sheep without thinking of it – often thought of as silly or stupid, Aggie Moo would become very heated and obstinate on this subject, to anyone who would dare imply they were, and argue that in fact sheep are very clever!

Always being surrounded by animals it was no surprise that I too craved for my own. My mother, not wanting anymore on her plate, flatly refused at first but unbeknown to me at the time, Aggie Moo was on my side negotiating that a cat for the surgery would be a good thing – hence my Tiggy cat came along, and later, as mentioned, a tortoise. A few years later, when without asking I saved up and brought myself a hamster, cage and all the accessories, my mother went apoplectic, marched me back to the pet store to return everything it was again Aggie Moo on my side. She thought it was a crying shame and felt so sorry for me that she gave me some of her childhood lead farm animals, a few of which I still cherish to this day.

After she retired and the surgery was sold, we all kept in close contact and she continued to treat Tiggy and later on our dog Simba. She lived on Streetly Lane with her sister Antoinette, and as my grandmother also lived on Streetly Lane, it became tradition that we would walk up and have tea together either on Christmas Eve or the Sunday before Christmas as even when she was retired she never stopped (it was no surprise that she kept up her voluntary work at the zoo even when we made murmurs of actually how safe her driving abilities were and as for her flight on her birthday, we didn't expect anything less!).

Our animals were always welcome and she would wave a hand of 'don't worry', as our puppy Simba happily chewed the horse hair from her chairs! As you can imagine, her stories were always wide and varied, I only wish I could remember them all now and look forward to hearing stories from other people.

I do remember Aggie Moo would sometimes talk of her brother, who was a pilot and died in the war.

It was always obvious that she was a true advocate of veterinary science and of women working in this field. As I grew up and went through school, although we didn't see each other as often and in some years, it would just be the Christmas visit, she never forgot birthdays or special occasions. When I had my daughters, she delighted in them as much as she had delighted in me as a young child. My only regret is that by then, I had moved away and so they only ever really saw her a few times; Birthdays, Christmases and when she held a party for her house when it reached its 100th birthday! She loved the huge wild garden there and delighted in the foxes that inhabited it.

My own mother fought and lost a brave battle with cancer six years ago and it was Aggie Moo who met me in the church and held my hand as we walked down the aisle behind her coffin and sat by my side throughout the service; something I will never forget.

The summer that she herself died we were arranging a summer tea party meet up, which unfortunately never happened. I feel her loss as keenly as I feel the loss of my mother and grandmother. I will always be grateful for knowing such an amazing lady and sharing the early years of my life with her.

To many, Mary Brancker was brusk and at times even rude, but to me, she will always be my 'Aggie Moo'. I am so very glad that she is being commemorated.

The Mary Brancker Bursary

When the Twycross Zoo Association (TZA) was asked to leave the zoo, we set up a similar organisation, the Independent Conservation and Wildlife Society, to be known as tza. We had a substantial amount of our own money to help us on our way.

Mary had always wanted to encourage and help students of animal based subjects and with this in mind, we decided to set up a bursary in her name to do just that. After much thought, Belinda (Belle) Bird came up with the idea of using her college (Brooksby Melton College) for this purpose. Her students are involved with animal behaviour, animal management and veterinary nurse studies, and after discussions with the Principal, the bursary was finally set up.

Students can apply to the bursary for a grant to help them with projects, or with their final thesis. The bursary will run initially for ten years, but this may be extended or moved if necessary.

When the day was fixed for the celebration of Mary's life, senior tutors from Brooksby were invited to hear more about this inspirational lady. Hazel Palmer from the college gave a brief description of what the bursary means to the students and said how delighted she was to be associated with such a respected lady as Mary.

Thanks from Brooksby Melton College for the Mary Brancker Bursary

Hazel Palmer from Brooksby Melton College was pleased to be associated with the celebrations held to commemorate the life of Mary Brancker.

She was equally pleased that the Mary Brancker Bursary had been set up for students at the college. The first student to benefit from this has completed her studies and the financial help has been very much appreciated. Other students will now be helped through the bursary, and as such the name of Mary Brancker will continue to be remembered.

The students who will receive the grants will be those studying animal based subjects, for example animal management, animal behaviour and those who wish to become veterinary nurses.

On behalf of the college, Hazel took the opportunity to thank the organisers once more for their help.

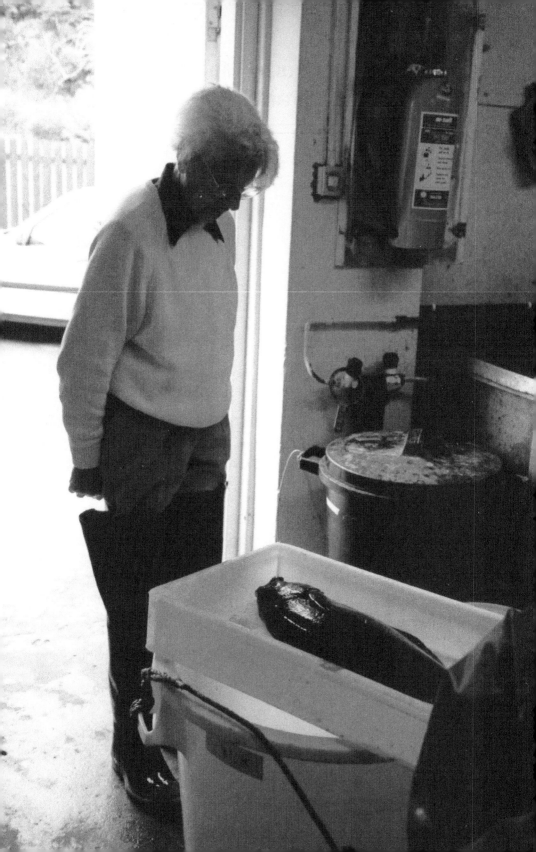

Memories from Victor Manton

Read on the day by Mark Ellis.

Like many others, a lasting memory I have of Mary is her infectious and all-pervading laugh. Nothing could douse that sound – nor the infectious pleasure emanating from the author. It must have been early 1963 when I first heard it and quickly made friends with the owner. Both then working in the zoo world, we joined the British Veterinary Zoological Society where eventually I served as Secretary to her time as President. That, of course, cemented our friendship and I began unveiling the background of such an outstanding veterinarian.

Coming from a large family as she was, she was, she always said, the dumbest member of it! Mary was devastated by the loss of a cousin (Sir Sefton Brancker – the Director of Civil Aviation) in the R101 airship crash in 1930 and of her brother Paul (DFC and Bar) killed in action in 1942. Never blessed with the best of health, she nevertheless managed to enjoy her activities with her younger relatives and indeed on one occasion was nearly drowned when a sailing dinghy capsized and she was left under the water trapped by the upturned sails.

Qualifying from the Royal Veterinary College in London in 1937, where she was one of the first women so to do, she joined the Lichfield Veterinary Practice of Henry Steele-Bodger where, due to the evacuation of the British Veterinary Association's headquarters to the same site on the outbreak of war in 1939, she became increasingly involved in veterinary politics. This eventually led to her appointment as President of that organisation in 1967 (the only woman to achieve this office until 2005). During this time, she suffered from constant and acute back pain and underwent a number of operations in attempts to cure the condition. All it achieved was to lumber her with metal plates and pins which, she used to enjoy telling her audience, set off numerous warning devices at airport security posts. Despite these disadvantages she still had managed to become a member of the Home Guard (Dad's Army) – horse mounted company – whose duties included patrolling

Sutton Park looking for parachutists!

In 1972, she published her book of experiences as a veterinary surgeon. This was entitled 'All Creatures Great and Small' and coincidentally released for sale at the same time as the James Herriot book of the same name!

Never one to push her name forward she was nevertheless appointed OBE in 1969 following her work during the foot and mouth outbreak of 1967/68. In 1977 she was awarded the Fellowship of the Royal College of Veterinary Surgeons, in 1996 she was awarded a Doctorate of Stirling University and in 2000 she was appointed CBE in the New Years' Honours of that year.

In her work Mary was never afraid to 'get her hands dirty' and was never more happy than when working with animals – perhaps especially if they were primates. Today when women form such a high proportion of veterinary surgeons, one can easily forget that Mary was in a tiny minority and shone a beacon of light to show that a woman could be as effective a veterinary surgeon as any man. At last she can rest in peace.

Memories from Mark Ellis

Two things stand out in Mark's memory about Mary.

The first was of the several visits Mary had with her former staff to the Zoo: Mary would be still striding out at the end of the day, whilst younger members were flagging several yards behind her.

He also recalled the day when he and his family were visiting the book stall at the zoo and he 'lost' his daughter. He suddenly heard laughter from beneath a table and realised that both Mary and his daughter were crawling around playing 'caught you'. Daughter was 2 years old, Mary was 90!

Memories from Jo Ellis

I was TZA Volunteer Co-ordinator and Mary (as she was known to members of TZA) was one of my volunteers. I can only recall hearing her called Winifred when meeting my mother. My mother, whose name was also Winifred Mary, was a little older than Mary and was also a TZA volunteer. When they greeted each other it was always 'Hello Winifred Mary', 'Hello Winifred Mary', both having cheeky grins on their faces.

Volunteering at Twycross Zoo was started in the 1980s by a few keen members of the Twycross Zoo Association, this developed into a very dedicated and knowledgeable group of people until its close in 2010.

Mary joined this group and was a great volunteer. She was always very reliable and willing to have a go at anything from blowing up giraffes (I mean inflating plastic ones), selling books, helping visitors and imparting some of her great knowledge to them – just to mention a few of her talents, although she always claimed to have no skills.

One day the residents of a nursing home were coming to visit the Zoo so I asked if anyone was free to help push wheelchairs. Yes, you have guessed, Mary was one of the first to offer help. There was however an ambulant member of the group so I asked Mary to help him. They had a great day - I don't think they saw much of the Zoo but they were nattering to one another all day and I'm sure he learnt a great deal.

Mary however occasionally went missing when on duty, but we would soon find her either talking to her old friend, Randy, a spider monkey, or causing uproar in the Chimp enclosure visiting her other great friend, Louis. Mary's wicked sense of humour would give us a good laugh during our busy volunteering day at the Zoo

On the day of the Celebration I was asked to read out a message from Mary's Godson, Paul, who always called her Polly. (You will find this message later in this book).

I also read a letter written to Mary from Miss Badham and Miss Evans on Mary's retirement as Zoo Vet, dated March 26th 1986:

Dear Mary,

We would both like to express our thanks and appreciation for your help and services over the past twenty three years.
Prior to this at Hints and elsewhere!

The change over will be strange but we do hope that you will be available for consultation and continue to serve on the Council of the Society.

Your knowledge and expertise with the animals has been of tremendous help and value over the years.

We hope you will continue to visit us as a friend, you will always be welcome.

Molly and Nathalie

We hope that the plate of "Asante" will remind you of the animals and all the things we have strived for together. The TV we would like to think, you will enjoy in your extra leisure time!!

Editors Note: Asante was the first gorilla to be born at Twycross, and is

still here at the zoo. The TV may have been Mary's first TV, and extra leisure time? Mary, leisure?

And finally, a poem sent to Mary by Helen and John:

Mary had a little lamb
His fleece was white as snow
And everywhere that Mary went
The lamb was sure to go

He followed her to work each day
The road was just the same
Until one day he realised
That all roads led to fame

Little lamb, little lamb
Where have you been?
I've been with Mary to visit the Queen
Little lamb, little lamb, what saw you there?

I saw some strange people
And dined on fine fare
Little lamb, little lamb,
How does it feel?

To be the President doesn't seem real
But whether the sun shines
Or whether it snows
I'm following Mary wherever she goes!

Memories from Paul Nicholson

Read on the day by Jo Ellis.

My early memories of Polly (as she was known to my family) revolve around summer holidays spent on my uncle's converted lifeboat on the River Deben in Suffolk. Sometimes she would be able to spend a fortnight on the boat, sometimes only a week and one time only a weekend when she was between assistants. Living and sleeping on a boat moored in the middle of a river gave her the chance to relax and unwind, though we did row ashore each day to check for any 'post restante' mail at the post office. The days were spent sailing or rowing near our mooring or cruising the length of the river.

On one occasion Polly joined my cousins in their sailing yacht and ventured out of the mouth of the river into the North Sea. The rusty bolts holding the keel gave way and the yacht capsized. Polly was thrown into the sea and I remember her telling me afterwards that she surfaced twice under the sail before managing to clamber onto the hull. Her English setter who was with them set off swimming briskly for Holland and had to be brought back by one of my cousins. During the subsequent rescue a parting towrope flicked her ear causing it to bleed profusely, and the local paper later reported that she had lost her ear.

Sometimes my mother and I would come to stay with her and her mother in Four Oaks and I would be allowed to join Polly on her visits. White knuckle rides around Sutton rivaled modern theme parks. On one occasion, while watching her operate on a dog in her surgery, I fainted and was unceremoniously dragged out into the hall, by her assistant. Quite rightly, the dog came first.

She always had a love of boats and while my children were growing up we had a succession of holidays on the canals. Canal locks can be very heavy to operate but she was never beaten.

Memories from Rowena Johnson

My memories of Mary stem from only the last twelve years of her life, but as with everyone she met, Mary made a lasting impression on myself, my daughter Ruth and indeed the rest of my family.

Ruth and I first heard Mary's name when we volunteered to help put up the Christmas Grotto at Twycross Zoo. It was the November that Mary's hip had just broken and she could not be there to do her usual jobs. Jo Ellis, who was responsible for the original idea of the fund-raising Grotto for the zoo, assembled a band of willing volunteers each November weekend and allocated the tasks required for the Grotto to be ready at the start of December. I think it would be November 1999, and as I am very bad at remembering people's names I was very hazy as to who the absent 'Mary' was. Jo, when giving out the tasks, would say "Mary normally does this – could you do it today please?". I can remember wishing two things at the time, one that we had visited the Santa's Grotto the previous year, because we both found it very hard to visualise what we were trying to achieve, and secondly, that I had half the energy of the mysterious 'young at heart' Mary!

The following year on a sunny November day, Jo was again allocating the necessary Grotto tasks, this time with Mary fit and well again. Jo called "Rowena, will you help Mary wash the wooden penguins"? By then I knew the iconic Mary and therefore knew that I had to get this job right – she did not suffer fools gladly – but we were at a zoo where Mary was a renowned vet, wooden penguins – what, why and where?! As it later became apparent, I had not been the only person who was having trouble with names, most unusually Ivan and Jo spent the first couple of years of our volunteering time at the zoo unable to remember my own and my daughters, and resorting in the end to referring to us as the 'two R's'. So perhaps it was really Ruth who should have been washing penguins which would later be used to point the direction through the zoo to Santa's Grotto…We will never know the answer to which of us it was meant to be, but I do know that washing these 20 penguins took a long time, as Mary wanted to know about me and I was interested in her and her career.

As conversation flowed back and forth, one of the most important friendships of my life began. Mary asked me about my work as a school librarian and I mentioned about children who suffer from dyslexia. Suddenly, I realised Mary had straightened her back and was staring at me as light dawned. She had never heard of the term 'dyslexia' but suddenly she understood why she, but not her siblings, had found it so difficult to begin the journey of learning to read and write.

During the next few years, which turned out to be quite difficult ones for me, I had Mary's friendship and interest coupled with her sensible support and advice.

Later, I was able to help her to a small degree when she naturally became concerned about what would happen to the Brancker family books when she died. There was no direct relative in the country to whom she could pass them on and although she was in contact with a cousin in America, I think, she felt the books belonged here. Much to my surprise, she asked my advice because she said that the family originally hailed from Lancashire. Luckily my parents were friends with the Deputy County Archivist, Jacquie Crosby, and I contacted her for advice. On hearing that the Branckers originate from Liverpool, which of course is now an authority in its own right and no longer part of Lancashire, Jacquie put Mary in touch with the Liverpool City archive department. Mary went up to Liverpool with some of the books and the archivist admitted that she had expected them to be 'run of the mill' material but was thrilled with what Mary offered to the department as they indeed were part of that city's rich history. Mary made a second journey to take all the texts and documents to be securely housed up there and was relieved that a proper solution had been found for the problem.

In the autumn of 2002, I was able to tell Mary that I had been at last successful in finding a post as a qualified school librarian. Since our move from Norfolk in 1998 I had been working in bookshops because of the scarcity of school library posts in the Leicestershire area. Imagine my surprise when Mary said that she knew the school, as her godson Paul Nicholson had been a boarder there. If his mother was not available on 'leave out' weekends, a system we still have, then Mary would go and collect Paul at half twelve on the Friday afternoon and bring him to Sutton for the long weekend holiday. Over the next couple of years I was able to get invitations to the school Open Days for both Mary and Paul to go back and have a look at the school and grounds as they are now.

As a librarian I was asked by the zoo to put in a library which the keepers could use when they were studying for additional qualifications. Particularly during the winter months, Mary and her friend Iris Filmer would prefer to help me in the library than be outside giving talks to visitors. We made a good team. I would organise where the books should go, and do the cataloguing and classification. Iris would sit and put the library stamp in the books and Mary would carry them to and from the shelves. All went well until one day when Mary decided that instead of having families of animals together eg. apes, it would be better if they were grouped according to the continent they originated from. I could see her point to a certain extent but I, as a librarian, was following classification rules – and what would you do with the majority of migratory birds, fish, whales etc. Better to follow the classification system which was given to us by London Zoo which allowed for duplication of species and new research – Mary conceded, disaster was averted!

Mary was born in the same year as my aunt and in both these women and in others of the same generation, I recognised a determination to work hard in life, to face up to whatever problems arose and to do your best in all situations even if it meant personal hardships and difficulties.

Perhaps this came from being brought up during the First World War by mothers who were often alone as the men were involved in war work. In their time, they were the generation who in their mid-twenties had to take over the men's work themselves, as Mary did, when the Second World War arrived. Somehow these women managed to cope with all that life threw at them and to emerge at the end of their working lives with their love of life and their sense of humour intact.

I used to like listening to Mary's wartime experiences when we had finished our volunteer work and would go into the Appleby Inn for a meal. It was there, I think, that she told us the story of her heart attack which she had kept quiet about for many years, only being forced to admit to it when her hip broke. Just as an aside here, when Mary had recovered from her hip operation, she was on more than one occasion heard to explain, "I did not fall and break my hip. My hip broke, and so I fell". She quite rightly felt it was important that people realised that if hips are weakened they can break, causing a person to fall.

But I digress: while in hospital with the broken hip, the doctors could see from the ECG that Mary had suffered a heart attack at some point in her life. You can just imagine an unsuspecting doctor approaching this little white haired old lady patient to see if he could get any further insight into what the machine was telling him. Mary related to us how at first she continued to deny it had taken place but then she realised that she was in grave danger of being considered as forgetful in her old age.

The stunned doctor suddenly got the facts he required, as Mary admitted that the heart attack had taken place in the mid 1950's when she was on Princes Street in Edinburgh. Realising what was happening to her, she leant against the nearest shop front until the pain had passed. When the worst was over she felt herself lucky to have survived and continued with whatever work she had gone up to Edinburgh to do. As she was only in her mid-fifties at the time, she attributed the attack to the amount of work she had been required to do with not enough sleep and always feeling hungry during the war, particularly in the later years when all the young able-bodied male vets had been needed to go abroad to work with the horses in the Far East.

I think Mary left the doctor in no doubt that she had made a full recovery from her heart attack and that she intended to do exactly the same from her broken hip – and as speedily as possible. I would imagine that she was one patient that he would not forget in a hurry.

Memories from Chris Chadbourne

Read on the day by Lesley Jarrett.

Mary Brancker had been a member of Soroptimist International of Sutton Coldfield since it was founded in 1945 and she maintained regular attendance at meetings almost up to the end. She was a much loved honorary member of our club.

In the 1930s it was almost unheard of for a woman to become a vet in what was then a heavily male-dominated profession. She had to overcome many objections to achieve her ambition but having qualified in 1937, she joined the Steele-Bodger practice. She became a very well-known institution in the local area, practising as a veterinary surgeon in Sutton Coldfield, Tamworth and Lichfield for many years. Her long and distinguished career was recognised by numerous awards. In 1967 she was elected as the first female President of the British Veterinary Association and for four decades afterwards she remained the only woman to serve in this capacity. In 1969 she was awarded an OBE for her work during the foot and mouth epidemic of 1967/8, when she had to liaise closely with Government departments to co-ordinate the response to the epidemic. Later, in 2000, she was honoured with a CBE for services to animal health and welfare. She was described in The Times as 'one of Tony Blair's women icons', for which her family pulled her leg unmercifully.

She had a special interest and passion for primates and the big cats. She worked closely for decades with the late Molly Badham of Twycross Zoo, developing and promoting animal welfare and was involved in numerous research projects. Until shortly before her death she continued to work as a consultant to Twycross and often went there, enjoying showing people around and talking about her beloved animals. Her interest in all living creatures extended to fish and insects. Although formally retired from regular veterinary practice, she continued to serve on various committees. Until recently she remained a member of the National Halibut Fishing Industry board, regularly attending meetings in Scotland and all over the UK.

She liked fast cars and continued to drive until she was 93. For her 95th birthday, she had her first flying lesson – in a two-seater aircraft – and there was a lovely photograph in the local paper showing her with an ecstatic smile.

Mary had a wicked sense of humour with a fund of hilarious stories to tell. At club meetings there were usually gales of laughter from the table where she was sitting. None of us will forget an occasion when she did a talk for us and described in minute detail how hazardous it is for a giraffe to give birth because of its long legs, and precisely what happens when a vet administers an enema to an elephant….

She was an astute woman of achievement who was an inspiration to other women to join the veterinary profession. She will be greatly missed by Sutton Coldfield Soroptimists and by her many friends.

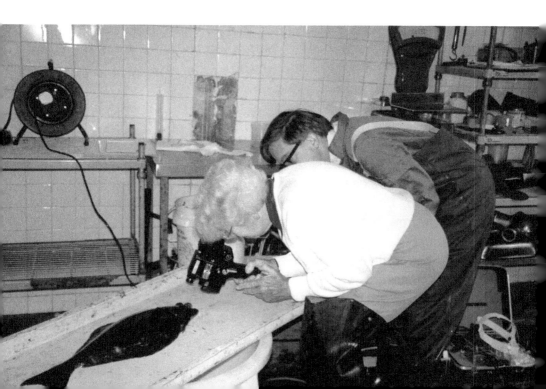

Memories from Tim Ellis

Mary always claimed not to be an expert – which, when you think about it is a good thing not to be, because it means you can turn your hand to a great many things rather than being given the same thing to do. Her willingness to explore new avenues is one of the things that always made Mary such an interesting person to talk to – she always had a wealth of stories to tell, but did not insist on dominating conversation.

Memories from Emma Sheardown

I have known Miss Brancker for about 20 years, meeting her at TZA meetings at Twycross Zoo.

My first memory of Miss Brancker was of me being an 'animal mad child' looking in awe at this kind, funny lady who used to be the zoo vet – Wow!!

I, like so many people (as I discovered at her memorial celebration) have so many personal memories of Miss Brancker.....I'll never forget on one Sunday at a TZA meeting, gearing up excitingly to ask her whether she thought with my disability if I could be a veterinary nurse – Mary's reply wasn't 'no'.....but 'let me go away and give it some thought' – as you can imagine, I waited eagerly for the next meeting to see what she had come up with!! A few weeks later she came back with a reply that resulted in me gaining a National Diploma in Animal Management.

During the summer holidays I, along with Mum and Dad, AB and Nan B used to spend a day with Mary at her home in Sutton Coldfield, we used to go for 'coffee'....but would sit round her dining room table, and coffee would turn into lunch...and lunch would turn into afternoon tea, etc, etc. I was always absolutely fascinated as we would sit listening to all her stories and experiences – she was amazing, a wealth of knowledge and experience, both in animal matters and veterinary science as well as life in general.

To me, her memorial celebration that we enjoyed just a few weeks ago was an extension of what we learnt and enjoyed sitting round her dining room table a few years ago, with the only difference being that it was other people telling the stories and jokes from various aspects of Mary's life – rather than Mary herself.

I can only describe the celebration as a unique afternoon in which people from a wide aspect of Mary's life shared their love and respect for this truly remarkable lady – I will always remember Miss Brancker with love and affection!

Editors Note: AB refers to Aunty Brit who is Barbara Brittain; Nan B was Winifred Mary Brittain, mother of Barbara Brittain and Jo Ellis.

Memories from Sue Bradley

When I wrote from Newcastle University's Centre for Rural Economy to ask Mary if she would consider making a recording about her life, she responded immediately, leaving a message on my answer phone. We knew she had been one of very few women to qualify as veterinary surgeons in the 1930s, and that her leadership as the first woman president of the British Veterinary Association during a major outbreak of foot and mouth disease had won life-long respect from the profession. I'd been encouraged to contact her as soon as possible – 'Mary is in her nineties' – but this was one of the clearest, most resonant voices I had ever heard. Her message was brisk and to the point. To my delight and gratitude, she was agreeing to the recording.

The first thing Mary did when we met was to take me to the pub for lunch. By the time we settled down to the interview, it felt like a shared enterprise. The recording was destined for the national oral history collection in the British Library, and would follow the in-depth life-story form which the Library uses to ensure that recordings will have maximum value to the wide range of listeners who consult what is essentially an audio social history archive. I asked Mary to talk about herself, including her early life and education, as well as her experiences of working as a vet from shortly before the Second World War.

We began in August 2009, I visited eight times over the following year, and the recording was still ongoing when Mary died in the summer of 2010. Her approach was considerate and extremely thorough – each time she would greet me with a fresh list of topics to include – and although she must often have been tired, she was reluctant to show it. "If you're coming all this way," she said, "it needs to be worthwhile."

How could it not be? Mary was the first interviewee in what has since become a partnership project with RCVS Knowledge (formerly the Royal College of Veterinary Surgeons Charitable Trust). Her involvement proved crucial to the project, not only because of her eminence in the profession but also because she cared about its history. As we walked back from the pub that day, she was already urging me to contact two former colleagues to invite them to take part. "I'll phone them up and tell them they must," she said. We all complied.

Mary's recording – of nearly twenty-five hours – makes a remarkable contribution to the historical record. Here are just a few of my personal highlights: Mary's memories of her father, who died when she was seven, but who had already researched the best boarding schools for his daughters' secondary education because the Branckers believed in educating girls. The pets Mary cherished as a child, including Toto the tortoise, who hid in the raspberry canes and spat at everyone but her. When Toto died, Mary's mother suspected an insect found on the animal, and sent a specimen to London Zoo, requesting a diagnosis. This would have been unusual in the 1920s, when pets generally didn't receive the attention they do today, but as Mary explained, her mother's family (the Eatons) considered animals to be almost as important as people. When Mary entered veterinary college, combining 'a proper education' with her interest in animals, both sides of the family were thrilled. There's Mary as a newly qualified vet going out alone to farms, where owners were suspicious of a woman until she proved her worth; or being allowed by her boss to sit 'on the edge of the circle' at meetings he held for heads of the profession to discuss veterinary policy during the Second World War. And, of course, I'd include some of Mary's acutely observed descriptions of animal behaviour, conclusive proof, if it were needed, of the enduring inspiration she found in her work. One of my favourites is her description of Louis the chimp at Twycross Zoo.

You can hear this, along with other extracts from Mary's recording, on the RCVS Knowledge website (See 'Early Interviews' and 'Education' pages):

Sue Bradley, Research Associate in Oral History, Newcastle University

Mary's recording formed part of a project entitled: Veterinary Lives in Practice oral history project (a collaboration between Newcastle University's Centre for Rural Economy and RCVS Knowledge, with the British Library as archive partner)

Excerpts from Letters

We received a number of letters in response to our request for memories about Mary; here, we have included excerpts from these letters:

"…I know little of Miss Brancker's exploits outside her professional life, but she was a skilful, caring and compassionate vet. In the summer of 1975, I carried my beloved young tabby cat, Sophie, who had smashed her jaw, covered in blood and barely breathing into Miss Brancker's surgery.

Sophie was heavily sedated, and I was told if she survived overnight to take her back the following day for surgery.

Not only did she survive that night, but for a further 13 very happy years – due to Miss Brancker's care"

Mrs Julie Douglas

A true lady.

She attended All Saints Church, Four Oaks, where I worship. Wednesday, the church was open for private worship and I was setting in for my hour stint. Mary was there cleaning and polishing woodwork. Putting on her coat at 3.30pm, I spoke to her.

"Finished Mary?" I asked.

"I'm never finished John" she answered.

What a lady!

J. J. Whyles

Miss Brancker had a veterinary practice in Sutton and as we were puppy walking for Guide Dogs for the Blind, we would have to take our puppy to her for regular check-ups. This I believe was work she did without payment. She was always very friendly to both us and the dogs.

Maureen Mander

[In] 1966, Miss Brancker taught my daughter, then aged 7 years old, to divide a pill and give it to her mouse to alleviate nervous problems. She had great patience with children.

During 1974-75, I taught at John Willimott Grammar School and organised the Duke of Edinburgh Award scheme for girls. I asked Miss Brancker if the girls could do Animal Care in the service section, at her practice. She could not have been more helpful. She and her staff took the girls through the course with great success.

In 1975-77, my daughter Kate volunteered and saw practice with Mary Brancker, who later gave her a reference on her application to vet college. Kate qualified at Liverpool and always had great respect for Mary Brancker. She was greatly admired in Sutton Coldfield as a vet and as a great character.

Pat Hovers

Archives

A hand drawn picture with accompanying poem:

On sticking needles into pigs
Our Coudah does excel
500 in a day she does
And twenty more as well
She's always in a tearing rush
With never time to spare
Her corners are quite special ones

Above Found in Mary's files, signed by an unknown 'Anne'

ROYAL VETERINARY COLLEGE.

Miss *W.M. Brancker* presented herself for the **A** Examination of the Royal College of Veterinary Surgeons in *July* and *passed*.

The marks awarded to her in each subject were as follows (maximum 100, pass minimum 45): Chemistry *55*, Biology *65*, Animal Husbandry *65*.

15 AUG 1933   193

_____ Principal

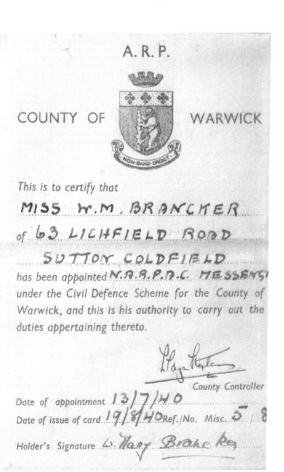

Above Mary passes one of her Royal College of Veterinary Surgeons exams.

Left Mary's warrant card from her wartime role as an Air Raid Precautions warden.

Ref:-B.5(53).

CHIEF CONSTABLE'S OFFICE,

WARWICK.

20th August, 1940.

To Miss W.M. Brancker, M.R.C.V.S.,

    63, Lichfield Road,

    SUTTON COLDFIELD.

AUTHORITY TO ACT UNDER REGULATION 79B OF THE
DEFENCE (GENERAL) REGULATIONS, 1939.

(General) Regulations, 1939, I hereby authorise you
W. M. Brancker, M.R.C.V.S., Veterinary Surgeon,
during, or within 12 hours after, the occurrence of hostile
attack in the vicinity, to slaughter any animal which appears
to you to be seriously injured and, if the animal is slaughtered
in a case to which the public have access, to remove the
carcase or cause it to be removed therefrom.

        Provided that you are not authorised to slaughter
any animal which appears to you to be neither at large nor
out of control or dangerous nor in such condition as to be
likely, in the circumstances, to cause public disorder or
disturbance, unless food suitable for human consumption would
be likely to be wasted if the animals were not slaughtered,
and the owner, if present, raises no objection.

Commander, R.N.,
Chief Constable of
Warwickshire.

Above Mary's authorisation from Warwickshire Constabulary to slaughter injured animals during the war.

All official communications to be addressed " The Chief Constable of Staffordshire, Stafford."

STAFFORDSHIRE COUNTY POLICE

Lt.-Colonel H. P. Hunter, C.B.E., D.L.
Chief Constable.
Telephone: Stafford 661 (four lines).

CHIEF CONSTABLE'S OFFICE,

STAFFORD.

5th September, 1940.

AUTHORITY TO ACT UNDER REGULATION 79B OF THE DEFENCE
(GENERAL) REGULATIONS, 1939.

To - Miss W.M.Brancker, MRCVS., 63 Lichfield Road,
Sutton Coldfield.

In pursuance of Regulation 79B of the Defence (General)
Regulations, 1939, I hereby authorise you, Miss W.M.Brancker,
during, or within 12 hours after, the occurrence of hostile
attack in the vicinity, to slaughter any animal which appears
to you to be seriously injured and, if the animal is
slaughtered in a place to which the public have access, to
remove the carcase or cause it to be removed therefrom.

Provided that you are not authorised to slaughter any
animal which appears to you to be neither at large nor out of
control nor dangerous nor in such condition as to be likely,
in the circumstances, to cause public disorder or disturbance
unless food suitable for human consumption would be likely
to be wasted if the animals were not slaughtered, and the
owner, if present, raises no objection.

Chief Constable of Staffordshire.

Above Mary's authorisation from Staffordshire County Police force to
slaughter injured animals during the war.

Above Mary with her godson Paul and his family, after receiving her CBE at Buckingham Palace in 2000

October 5th 1966

Miss W.M. Brancker, M.R.C.V.S.,
63, Lichfield Road,
Sutton Coldfield,.

Dear Mary,

Congratulations on your election as Junior Vice-President of the B.V.A. You have created history in being the first woman to hold this position, and I hasten to express the confidence which I place in you. This causes me some embarrassment as in addition to your charm and beauty I now have to concede that you have a modicum of brain.

With all good wishes,

Yours sincerely,

Rufus x x.

Above Mary receives a congratulatory letter from a Mr Bowden, on her appointment as Junior Vice-President of the British Veterinary Association.

81

GREETINGS TELEGRAM ✻

$A202 AP8 2.58 FOUROAKS BM 26 ALLPURPOSE

MISS W M BRANKER PRINCE OF WALES HOTEL

SOUTHPORT

= CONGRATULATIONS WILL YOU STILL NEED US WILL

YOU STILL FEED US WHEN WERE 64 FROM 63 +

Above A telegram believe to have been received from her staff at her practice at 63 Lichfield Road, however the date and occasion are unknown.

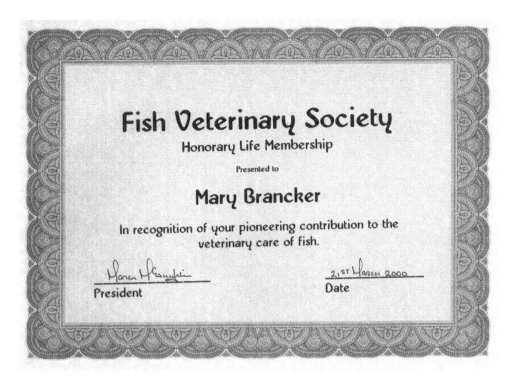

Above Mary's Certificate of Honorary Life Membership to the Fish Veterinary Society.

ROYAL COLLEGE OF VETERINARY SURGEONS

The

Francis Hogg Prize
for the Year 1965 was awarded to

Miss Winifred Mary Brancker

26ᵗʰ day of May 1965.

President

Secretary and Registrar

Above Mary receives the Francis Hogg Prize from the Royal College of Veterinary Surgeons in 1965.

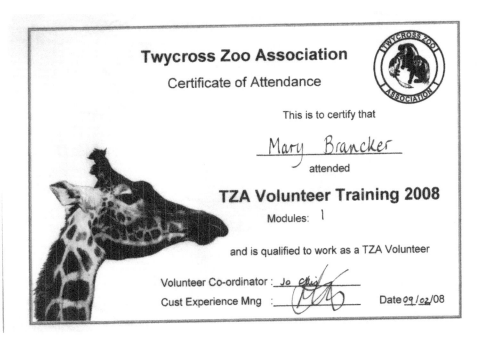

Twycross Zoo Association

Certificate of Attendance

This is to certify that

Mary Brancker

attended

TZA Volunteer Training 2008

Modules: 1

and is qualified to work as a TZA Volunteer

Volunteer Co-ordinator : Jo _____

Cust Experience Mng : _____   Date 09/02/08

Twycross Zoo Association

This Certifies That

Mary Brancker

Has completed two thousand minutes of Volunteer Duty during the year 2000, and is therefore awarded this

Diploma

Friday 1st December 2000

_____ President   _____ Chairman

Top Mary's Certificate of attendance from training undertaken as part of Mary's role in the Twycross Zoo Association in 2008.

Bottom Mary's Certificate of completion of 2000 volunteer hours for the Twycross Zoo Association in the Year of the Volunteer, 2000.

Resources

Veterinary Record Obituary: Peter Scott, Derek Lyon, Mike Fielding, Ian Keymer and Victoria Roberts, Veterinary Record, July 24, 2010, vol 167, p 145, accessed through the Royal College of Veterinary Surgeons, Council Meeting Minutes from Thursday, 4 November 2010 at http://www.rcvs.org.uk/document-library/council-papers-november-2010/

Fourth Supplement to the London Gazette Tuesday 24th January 1942: https://www.thegazette.co.uk/London/issue/35430/page/395/data.pdf

Wellington Roll of Honour: Military Archive Wellington Roll of Honour available at: http://lib.militaryarchive.co.uk/library/WWII/library/Wellington-Roll-of-Honour-1939-1945/files/assets/basic-html/page79.html

Commonwealth War Graves Commission – Commemoration Certificate for Henry Paul Brancker: http://www.cwgc.org/find-war-dead/casualty/2620267/BRANCKER,%20HENRY%20PAUL

Royal College of Veterinary Surgeons Knowledge (Oral History project) with extracts from Mary's recording:
http://knowledge.rcvs.org.uk/grants/awards-made/collaborations/capturing-life-in-practice
http://knowledge.rcvs.org.uk/grants/awards-made/collaborations/capturing-life-in-practice/education/

British Library Sound and Moving Image Catalogue (for the full recordings of Mary for the oral history project): cadensa.bl.uk and search for 'Mary Brancker'.

British Veterinary Zoological Society – the Zebra Foundation: http://www.bvzs.org/zebra-foundation

British Veterinary Association Awards: http://www.bva.co.uk/About-BVA/BVA-Awards/

The Telegraph - Mary Brancker Obituary: http://www.telegraph.co.uk/news/obituaries/medicine-obituaries/7919515/Mary-Brancker.html

The Independent – Mary Brancker Obituary: http://www.independent.co.uk/news/obituaries/mary-brancker-the-first-woman-president-of-the-british-veterinary-association-2051209.html

The Guardian – Mary Brancker Obituary:
http://www.theguardian.com/education/2010/aug/27/mary-brancker-obituary

Nicky Vincent – History of Women Veterinarians in Veterinary Online: http://www.vetsonline.com/publications/veterinary-times/archives/n-43-32/history-of-women-veterinarians.html

CPSIA information can be obtained at www.ICGtesting.com
Printed in the USA
LVOW05s1916230115

3856LVUK00010B/49/P